MW01076274

WORKING IN

MULTICULTURAL TEAMS

A biblical and practical guide

for team leaders and members

Johan Linder

WORKING IN MULTICULTURAL TEAMS:
A biblical and practical guide for team leaders and members

ISBN 978-1-5206124-5-4

Acknowledgements

This book is a team effort with contributions from people who have all helped.

My thanks go to Trix for editing and setting it out to finally get it printed, and to Nate for designing the book cover.

Then there is also a whole group of people from the OMF team who have been involved in editing, feedback and contributing stories - Sarah, Steve, Christine, Sheron, Kym, Gemma, Anna, Mike and Joyce. Thank you so much for your input, direction and advice.

Introduction

A Compelling Witness

I was the leader of a multicultural team in Bangkok for a number of years. The team members were serving all around Bangkok in various different kinds of work, and we would meet together once a month to pray and encourage one another.

At our monthly meeting, I invited a Thai pastor to share with us and he began by asking everyone to read from the Bible. To my surprise, everyone in the team had decided to bring the Bible along in their own language.

The pastor had assumed that everyone would have a Bible in Thai and read from that – but since some of them were still learning the local language, they found that difficult. I thought that everyone would bring the Bible in English because that was the language we usually used for our team meetings. We were surprised that each person had brought along their Bible in their mother tongue.

We decided that the best thing to do was for each person to read a verse in their own language. So we read the Bible in

Portuguese, Malay, German, Thai, Afrikaans, English and Korean. Some people might have been annoyed that they could not understand most of the words that were being read, but this experience opened my eyes.

I was amazed by the diversity of our team and that God would bring us all from different corners of the globe to be working together in Thailand to share the good news of Jesus with Thai people.

Multicultural teams are becoming more common both in the business world and the Christian world. Our world is changing. More and more people are moving from one country to another, from one side of the world to the other – and people from different cultures need to work together on many levels. Large numbers of Indians are moving to parts of the Middle East, some Middle Eastern people are going to Europe, Chinese people to Africa, Latin Americans to the USA. Some vibrant churches in Europe are now full of people born outside of Europe.

These areas of the world have changed – and the churches within them have changed. All these changes can make the teams that lead them more diverse and complicated.

With these complexities have come new opportunities. God is at work as people groups are moving to new places. People from some of the most unreached people groups can now be reached as they move to countries where they come into contact with Christians – such as the large numbers of people from Islamic countries leaving war-ravaged countries in Africa and the Middle East to live in Western countries more open to the gospel.

Conversely, Christians who have migrated to live and work in countries that are more closed to the gospel have opportunities to share about Christ – such as the large numbers of Filipino Christians in the Middle East, Taiwan and other countries where Jesus is not known.

Such large movements of people mean that Christians can introduce the previously unreached to Jesus. For Christians living in the host country, this means not having to learn a new language, or cope with changes in climate and food! However, we still need to be culturally sensitive and informed and know about the people that we are trying to engage with the message of Jesus.

To do this well, we need to work in multicultural teams.

Working in multicultural teams is harder than we may expect. We all bring with us many ways of thinking and doing things that seem normal to us, but may seem strange to people from other cultures. On top of that we all bring hidden expectations and values from our home cultures. These only show themselves as we work side by side over a period of time. Our cultural expectations can be like land mines that sit under the surface and only blow up when they are stepped on.

Knowing how to work with people from other cultures is difficult and can make us feel very uncomfortable. We can disagree over how decisions are made, what the leader should do, how the team should work, what good table manners are, how to dress, how to share an opinion – an unexpected explosion can destroy a team.

Sometimes we will feel offended by others because they are doing things differently. When this happens, our first reaction is to think, "That's wrong!" because our own culture has told us that it is not right to do things in that way. All our lives, our culture has told us the "right" way to do things.

Then we are faced with people who don't do it that way, because their culture has taught them to react in a different way. We want to say, "That's wrong!" However, being too quick to judge something as "wrong" can be very dangerous. It can make people defensive and cause division.

Thankfully, God has graciously given Christians the resources to handle these challenges. He has forgiven us in Jesus in spite of our rebellion and weaknesses. This helps us to forgive others and seek to work with them. The Holy Spirit helps us overcome division, conflict and mistrust. The Bible gives us practical guidance, instruction, and encouragement.

This doesn't mean that multicultural teams are easy for Christians. I have not written this book because I have found a way to make it easy – or because I have been successful in working well within multicultural teams.

I have, however, worked in multicultural teams – and made many mistakes. I didn't know about some of these mistakes until months or years later. Some of those lessons were painful. But I have also known the joys of working alongside my Christian brothers and sisters from all over the world. These experiences have changed me and opened up a whole new understanding of how God has made people different.

While multicultural teams are challenging, as Christians we are compelled to work well within them. God shows Himself powerfully through teams who mutually respect each other and genuinely love each other.

An effective multicultural team can be a visual witness to the power of Jesus – showing that our commitment to God is more important than our national identity. This can be spiritual dynamite and has the power to transform communities. An effective multicultural team can break down hostility and factions between cultural groups in the host culture. They can be a shining example of God's new community in Jesus.

The early Christians were careful to be inclusive of all cultures and nationalities. If this had not happened, then Christianity would still be a small sect within the Jewish religion.

When the Grecian Jewish widows complained about not receiving their fair share of food rations, the apostles made sure that this problem was addressed (Acts 6). The Council of Jerusalem was a historic decision to formally include Gentiles in the Christian faith without imposing Jewish rules and regulations on them (Acts 15).

When Peter distanced himself from the Greeks, Paul publicly rebuked him for withdrawing from them (Galatians 2:11-21). Paul spoke powerfully against those who wanted to impose their Jewish identity on the early church (Philippians 3:2). It is clear that accepting people from all nationalities and cultures is an important teaching of the New Testament.

When people from different cultures find it hard to work together, it can be easy to withdraw. We are tempted to think, "If working together is so hard, then isn't it more efficient to work with people from the same culture?"

the easy way out

It might be efficient – but we must ask, is *efficiency* what God desires for His church? God's goal is for people from all tongues and nations to be gathered together before Him in right relationship with Him and with one another. Those who are saved will worship Him with the same song, "Salvation belongs to our God, who sits on the throne, and to the Lamb." (Revelation 7:9-10)

When we form a team of people from different cultures, we take a deliberate step towards God's goal of bringing together a great multitude from every nation, tribe, people and language.

If you are reading this book, it may be that you have already come up against the struggle of working alongside others in multicultural team. This is normal – so don't give up!

A person who works in a multicultural team becomes a witness and a leader. You have a responsibility to God and to the people in your community. You show that a Christian multicultural team can work. They can work because God is with you and helping you. You show that Jesus has the power to overcome cultural differences, that you have something bigger and more important to follow than your nationality or cultural rules. They can work because the multicultural team is vital to declaring God's love to all people.

9

Just as Jesus prayed, "May they be brought to complete unity to let the world know that you sent me and have loved them even as you have loved me." (John 17:23)

But what does this look like? How do Bible-based multicultural teams work in practice?

This book aims to look at the most common issues that face multicultural teams, and better equip team members and leaders to deal with them. If you are working together with people from another culture then this book can help you.

It doesn't matter whether you are a team leader or simply working together with someone from another culture. There are many principles in this book which will help you to be a little more aware of some of the differences that can arise when you try to be a "team" together.

Our attitude is really important because it will have a huge effect on our relationship with other team members as we engage and interact with them.

Our spiritual resources will come into play when we come into difficult issues.

How team members come into the team is also important and can determine how well they are able to contribute.

How decisions are made and communicated can vary a lot between cultures and can be a source of conflict and misunderstanding. Once open conflict breaks out, it can be very difficult to resolve.

Changes in teams can upset the balance in the relationships that have developed, which means that the process of restoring a new balance needs to start all over again.

As you can see, it can be really hard work – and it is important to walk into a team with a humble attitude of serving God and each other.

I hope that this book will be helpful to anyone who works in a multicultural team. It might be a church leadership team, an international team working on a project, even a team working in a missional business.

I have written this book not only for leaders – I hope that this will be a useful resource for a *whole team* to read together, and that it will help each team member discuss the implications of what they have learned.

Above all, I hope that it will equip you to honor God in the way that you are able to work together with other people who love Him and want to share His love.

Chapter 1

Our Attitude to Diversity

Over the years I have worked with many teams. Some of these have been able to work together for a long time and others have descended into conflict.

What makes a difference is whether there has been a deliberate choice to work together – even though there are differences in theology, expectations, strategies and personalities.

Those who have succeeded in a multicultural team have been *those who have committed to rejoicing in how God has made us all different and diverse.*

The ones that did not last showed increasing negativity at people's differences, and an increasing frustration that their own expectations and desires were not being met.

We can choose to see cultural diversity as an asset or a problem. It can be a great gift from God to grow our understanding and appreciation of other cultures. Or it can be a heavy burden which gets in the way of our work.

If we see diversity as a problem, our attitude will break down trust and create tension in relationships.

Others will notice our disapproval in our body language and tone of voice, that we see them as a problem to be solved, that we see them as people who need to change to be more like us – even if we don't say it out loud.

When trust is lost even small issues can break down unity so that working together is impossible.

On the other hand, if we see diversity as an asset, we will rejoice that we are different – and others will notice that we see them as people with valuable thoughts and ideas.

When we see cultural diversity as something to be treasured, our attitude will speak louder than words, and can overcome all language barriers.

Case study: Old enemies in history, new allies in Christ

A local health project in Southern China had a team which consisted of a Chinese, Japanese and Korean. While all from Asian cultures, at different times their countries had also fought one another. Some of their cultural values and ways of working together were quite different. They did not find it easy to work together. They had disagreements and misunderstandings.

But they persevered. They were all Christians and had made the commitment that they would work together and bring this project to completion.

After a few years, a local person who had been watching the team at work made an observation. He said that he was so impressed by the way that they had been able to work together in love in spite of their differences. He had seen some of the disagreements they had faced.

But he had also seen them work through those disagreements in love and humility. And they had worked as a team in spite of their different personalities and backgrounds. He saw how even people from nations with long histories of conflict and hurt could learn to love and respect each other through God's power. This was a powerful testimony to the power of Jesus to change lives.

Starting off well: Building a positive attitude to diversity

Often we can become judgmental when we interpret people's actions according to our own belief system. It is therefore really important that our attitude is a positive one, where we treat everyone in the team as a friend without judging them or their actions.

Volunteers make up the team

When we begin a new multicultural team, it is important that everyone commits voluntarily to becoming a member of that team. It is hard to work in a multicultural team, so you need to have people on board who have made a wholehearted commitment to be there. Being coerced or ordered to work together is a poor foundation for building the perseverance needed to overcome difficulties.

Taking time to build relationships and talk through vision and strategy before the team comes together is a worthwhile investment. This will help potential members to own the vision of what the team is working towards.

A couple from Canada were sent to work together on a local project in South East Asia in a multicultural team. There was little consultation before the team came together and there was little or no preparation before the team was formed. As a result, the team members felt that they hardly knew each other before they were expected to work together.

The Canadian couple became increasingly frustrated at what they felt was a lack of clarity and direction in the team. A few months later the Canadian couple left the team and returned home feeling very disappointed that all the teams they had worked in during their 4 years had fallen apart.

A fixed period of time

The commitment of each member of the team for an agreed amount of time is useful to make it work in the long term. You are not marrying your team, so it doesn't have to be a life-long commitment! It can be only for a few weeks, months or years.

Giving people an option of renewing when the initial period is completed is often helpful. This allows people to move on without any shame, or to continue if they desire to. It can also be very helpful for leadership to not renew someone's place on the team if they are not suitable to continue.

Dom and Fran were sent to work in a church planting team for 2 years. They were happy to take on the assignment and worked well with the team leader and another single worker for a year. They felt that after the 2 years, they could continue to work with the team for another 4 years.

Then another experienced worker returned to the team, who had a very different style of working, and changed the direction of the work. This made Dom and Fran quite uncomfortable. They were able to continue for another year, but when they finished their 2-year commitment, they requested a transfer to another team.

This was organised without any bad feelings on either side, and they were able to part as friends. Having a clear time commitment provided a way out to work in another team without tension or conflict.

New words for old ideas

Often there will be misunderstandings in a team which can cause frustration. When this happens, it is important not to become angry and frustrated. Often the misunderstanding was caused by lack of language or not understanding a concept, not because of a deliberate intention to cause hurt. Reacting badly can spoil the relationship.

Sometimes when there are different cultural expectations we need to think up new ways of dealing with the tension. If we realise that there is an ongoing issue that causes misunderstanding and confusion then it may be helpful to invent a new language or procedure which will help make things clearer.

In our organisation the words "supper" and "dinner" refer to different meals during the day depending on who you talk to. For those booking into a meal at the guest house, this often became very confusing when people would turn up for a meal expecting to eat, when food had not been prepared for them.

To clear up this confusion, everyone had to agree to use new words when they were booking in for a meal, and use the terms "midday meal" and "evening meal."

Recognising our own values – and others' values

When we are in our own culture, we are like fish who don't even notice the water we are swimming in. We think that everyone swims in the same water.

It is not easy to talk about our values when we assume other people are just like us. But we do think differently – about work, the way we bring up our children, what we do with our free time, what we expect of our leaders, how strict we are about time, or how friendships work.

Because we think differently, the relationship can confuse us. When conflict happens, we often want to find out who is to blame. Sometimes we blame ourselves. Sometimes we blame others. It is usually not helpful to look for someone to blame. It is better to try and find out where there is a lack of understanding.

One of the challenges of working in a multicultural team is that we often do not find out what the conflicts will be until the team comes together and tries to work together. But if we recognise at the start that we come together with different values, this can help ease our own confusion.

Case study: Value clashes within multicultural teams

Jim had joined a volunteer team which taught free English classes as part of an outreach to South-East Asian people. The team of teachers consisted of both English speakers and South East Asians. After working with the team for 3 years, Jim said he had enough. "I don't like these people – they never tell the truth!"

He'd come from a European cultural background that encouraged people to be direct and straightforward when talking to people. He found it hard to work with South East Asians, who sought to avoid causing offense by saying what they thought the other person wanted to hear.

Whether or not they were telling the direct truth was less important than the relationship. They would only tell their true thoughts and feelings once they felt safe with another person. They did not want to be dishonest or to deceive anyone.

Jim could not adapt to this way of thinking, and left the team. He felt that telling the truth was more important than maintaining a harmonious relationship.He could not, or did not want to understand the people that he was working with and why they acted as they did. If he had done so, then he would have opened himself to saying things in a way that would not offend people quite so much.

Values and expectations that can cause tension

Team

What it means to be a team varies greatly from one person to another. In some cultures, it might mean doing everything together – and to others, it might mean only meeting together to share ideas once in a while.

It is important that expectations are clear from the beginning so that some people are not disappointed when they realise that their expectations of the team are not being met.

Time

Some cultures think that time and efficiency are very important – and others tend to think that it is more important not to rush things and keep good relationships.

This can cause frustration when some feel that team members are wasting others' time. It can also work the other way when some feel that the others concentrate too much on being efficient and on time at the expense of relationships.

Directness

Some cultures value honesty. This can lead them to be very direct in expressing their views and feelings.

Others value relationships and harmony. In these cultures people are taught to keep their views and feelings to themselves and only share what they really think when it is "safe" with people that they trust.

Because of this cultural programming, some people can come across as timid and shy when they are not, and others can cause hurt and offense because of their directness.

Power Distance

Some cultures are very respectful of their leaders and would never speak against them in a group. Other cultures want to treat their leaders just like everyone else.

Imagine the tension when a team member openly questions or disagrees with the leader in front of the group. Or if a team member feels that she cannot disagree with a bad decision which is going to affect the whole team.

Work and Leisure

Some cultures have a clear distinction between work and leisure time – while for others it is all part of a whole. This might mean that some team members have an expectation of spending time together after work is finished, while others don't.

The kinds of things that people like to do in their spare time also vary widely. Some like playing or watching sport, some like shopping, some like watching movies, some like to be alone, and some like to be with friends.

Family

The way that families operate varies greatly from one culture to another – and this can influence the team.

What time do you put children to bed? Are they included in the team activities and events? What do you feed children and when? How strict are you and how do you enforce discipline?

It can be very upsetting to be criticised for the way that we bring up children.

Money

The way that money is used and spent can cause tension within a team. Some people may have different priorities on how the money is spent and the reasons for it.

It is important that this is resolved well and that clear policy is developed.

Church

This is especially important in Christian teams that have a ministry focus around church.

In a multicultural team, there will be different perspectives on how to run a church, the elements of a good service, the type of music, how prayer is done, the type of governance, and the roles of women and the pastor.

There needs to be understanding of how the team members will work together in all these areas.

Leadership

The expectations of what the leader should do vary widely from one culture to another.

In some cultures the leader is expected to be very directive. In other cultures the leader is expected to be a facilitator and a friend. What is considered to be good leadership in one culture may be inappropriate in another.

Even the way that team members show and give respect to the team leader may be quite different as well.

It is important to try to work out what these underlying expectations are, and how the leader can respond to them.

It may be that some team members will need to change their expectations, and develop some new ones in line with other team members and the natural working style of the leader.

Case study: Friendships and expectations

John and Sally had been working with their team for over 3 years. It had not been easy, but over time, the 6 team members learned to work together and reach out to their community.

The 3 men on the team worked together well, made many contacts and developed relationships, and people were becoming interested in giving their lives to Jesus. The women, however, found working together more difficult. They came from different cultural backgrounds, had different expectations of friendship, and found it hard to open their hearts to each other. One of the women, Sally, decided to try and talk to one of the other women, Florence, about this.

It did not go well. As they talked, Sally found that Florence became more and more defensive and reluctant to be open. Florence's family and home culture had not encouraged people to share their feelings openly, so this was something that was very frightening to her. By the end of the conversation, Sally felt that their relationship was no better than before.

At the next team meeting, the atmosphere was even more tense. Sally could not understand why Florence was so distant.

Knowing about other cultures personally

Just knowing how things "work" in each culture can help a lot in building trust and overcoming barriers.

Many conflicts can be avoided and resolved if we have knowledge about cultures that are not our own.

It is not easy to find out this information because some things can only be learned through experience – from actually interacting cross-culturally.

I wish I'd known more about eating food with Koreans before talking about business, or about fun and joking around when meeting with Brazilians.

As we work with other cultures, we'll begin to understand some of the points of tension and learn how to avoid them before they damage our team.

And as more and more people work in multicultural teams, our collective pool of knowledge will grow.

Being slow to judge and quick to clarify

We can expect there to be times when people will offend us and we will offend others. When things happen that disappoint or offend us, it is easy to think it's because someone else has done the wrong thing.

Sometimes our family or close colleagues agree with us (because they too come from our culture), and it can be very difficult not to judge people when they do things we would not accept in our own culture. But we need to accept that doing things differently is not necessarily "wrong."

Our co-workers may have broken the rules of our culture, but what they did may be acceptable and even appropriate in their own culture – and vice versa. It is important to not judge quickly, to maintain a positive attitude towards working in a multicultural team, and to learn from these circumstances.

An example of this is simple table manners. In some cultures it is perfectly acceptable to make loud noises when you eat your food. In some cultures people should not talk with their mouths full, and when they eat they should do so quietly. In other cultures, it is fine to talk with your mouth full and to make slurping noises when drinking and munching noises when chewing.

When we are with other people who have a different way of eating it can be irritating.

There are all kinds of other things about eating that can cause conflicts – such as where do you eat and at what time, who should pay the bill when you are finished, how to treat children at the table, what utensils to use, how much to serve, where to place people, what is the appropriate thing to wear, what to talk about. The list goes on.

Case study: East and West and inter-generational differences

Sam had a job working for the English-speaking congregation of a church made up of Chinese immigrants and their children. While the adult congregation spoke in Chinese, the English congregation was mainly made up of children and young people, and Sam was only a few years older than most of the people he was ministering to. The other Chinese pastors were much older.

One time in a leader's meeting there was a discussion about church finances and how to raise money. One elder thought that it would be a good idea to have a church fete selling things in order to make money. Sam had never felt that the time and energy put into running a fete was worth the amount of money that was raised. He spoke out against the idea.

After some more discussion the idea was again raised and Sam spoke against it using the same argument as before.

The following Tuesday, the Chinese pastor called Sam into his office to talk. As they sat down, he sighed deeply and said, "You are so young." Then he said it again.

Sam knew by this stage that he had done something offensive and apologised, even though he was not sure what he had done wrong. They prayed together and Sam walked out of the Chinese pastor's office still not clear about what he did to cause offense.

It took quite some time for him to work out that the Chinese elders had probably been offended when he spoke against the church fete. In Sam's own culture, it would have been appropriate for someone of his age and position to say what he did – but in a Chinese context, it had been offensive to the older people in the room. He realised that he had a lot to learn about working in another culture.

Questions for personal reflection

How important is working in a multicultural team to you?

What do you see are the advantages of working in a multicultural team?

What do you think are some of the disadvantages?

Things to do. . .

As a team

Spend time talking together about vision, strategy, goals, roles, expectations and basic values (before a commitment is made to work together!)

For team leaders

With each team member, set a time period for the commitment to work together. Agree to evaluate and make a new commitment after that time.

For team members

Interview someone from a different culture about how they perceive people who come from your culture. Ask them about their culture and what they see as strengths and weaknesses among their people. Try to find out what they admire about your people, the things that they don't like, and what they see as the main challenges in working with you and your people group.

Chapter 2

Our Spiritual Resources

A few years ago, I was the leader of a small team working together to reach out to Buddhist people in our community. I was not very experienced, but I enjoyed being the leader of the team.

After a year or so, an experienced couple returned to the team after a year away. Because they were older and had previously been the team leaders, they came back with the expectation that they would once again be leading the team.

At first this was very difficult, because it meant that the direction and goals that I had set for the team were no longer relevant. They had their own ideas about where the team was going and kinds of things that we should be focusing on.

It was really hard to let go of leading the team, but in the end I realised that it is ultimately God that we are accountable to, and to fight for my will to be done would have created division.

I decided that the best thing to do was to let go of trying to be the leader and become a good follower instead. It worked – and our team developed a level of closeness and friendship that we did not have before.

If Jesus truly is the King of kings and the Lord of lords, then surely His people can unite together under His name! We belong to the same kingdom, and we are going to spend eternity together, so it is important that we learn to work together now.

Christians bring some resources that are unique and which can help to bring people from different cultures together.

What are these resources and how can they help us?

The Holy Spirit

When Jesus left this earth to prepare a place in heaven for us, He did not leave us alone. He left the Holy Spirit to empower those who believe in Him. The Holy Spirit is a Person who dwells with us and in us. He gives us the power to live a life for God.

The first sign of that power was the ability to communicate across language barriers (Acts 2:1-13). This was the first and most important activity of the early Christians. They were to take the message of God's glory in the resurrection of Jesus to other nations and cultures.

From then on, the followers of Jesus were not to think that belonging to God's kingdom was restricted to only the Jewish race. The right to enter God's kingdom is now a right for all those who love and follow Him.

To prove this, God gave His Spirit to a Gentile centurion (Acts 10). The idea that God would accept people as His own children from outside the Jewish race was not a new thought in the Jewish Scriptures, but it took a lot of convincing before the early church accepted that this was God's will. (Acts 11:18).

In a multicultural team of Christian workers, there is a bond with Jesus which is greater than any allegiance to a nation or cultural group. Jesus is now the Head, and we need to submit to His will. As Christians, we are now part of the new kingdom of God, which takes priority over our culture.

This can be a difficult process and will require us to let go of some things that we feel attached to. God has given us new life which we do not deserve. He has forgiven us for all our wrongs and our rebellion against Him through Jesus' death. We have humbled ourselves and turned our lives around to follow Jesus.

The Holy Spirit is a witness to this change. Sometimes we mistake an outgoing personality with the Holy Spirit's power. The Holy Spirit's power, however, is consistent with the fruits of the Spirit – love, goodness, kindness, gentleness, and self-control.

These help us to overcome conflicts with people from different cultures – to show humility and meekness, not demanding that things are done the way we want.

When we walk in the Spirit, God enables us to cross over cultural boundaries. It becomes possible to bring people from all nations and cultures together as one body as we serve Jesus Christ together.

Grandma Bun had been a Thai Buddhist all her life. She had never had much to do with foreigners before, but when her daughter invited her to go to a house meeting to find out more about Jesus she decided to attend.

She had always thought that foreigners were quite rude, outspoken and aggressive – but when she went along to the meeting, she found something quite different. The people in the group sung songs to God, they read from the Bible and they prayed for one another.

What struck her more than anything was that these people really cared for one another – and they cared for her as well. They shared openly about their struggles, and they showed genuine love and interest in helping. She had never come across this before – and it made a real impact on her life.

After attending the group for a few weeks, Bun shared about a problem in her life and the group prayed for her – she cried as she felt the touch of the Holy Spirit in her life.

As she was leaving, the leader reminded her of God's love for her. With a stunned look on her face, she said, "Yes, I realise how much God loves me now!"

God's Word

As citizens of God's kingdom we have God's word to show us how we can live together from our diverse backgrounds.

It has always been God's plan that all nations would be blessed through Abraham (Genesis 12:1-3), and we see this coming true in Revelation, where people from all nations are gathered before Him singing His praises.

It is His word that makes this happen in people's lives.

In our team meetings, we would usually start by reading a section of God's word together. We would then discuss how the text might apply to our lives and finish by praying about what God had said to us through His word.

It is amazing how often God would be speaking and convicting our team members of various sins, as well as encouraging each of us to live holy and godly lives. We have seen people confess their discouragement, pride, being judgmental of others in the team and the local culture, addictions such as pornography, feelings of anger, failure and guilt.

The word of God is also able to change cultures and transform people to reflect His glory.

We would not have the worldwide church we have today without the understanding that God welcomes people from all cultures into His Kingdom. The Bible tells us God showed Peter that Samaritans (Acts 8:17) and Gentiles could also receive God's Spirit, just as the Jews had (Acts 10-11). The church later had to make some policy decisions about the expectations that the church was to place on Gentile believers (Acts 15:28).

Working in multicultural teams

The early Corinthian church was composed of people from very different cultures, statuses and languages coming together (1 Corinthians 12:12).

The Galatian church had to learn the importance of different racial groups living and working together, rather than separating themselves from each other, as Peter had been doing (Galatians 2:14).

The Ephesians needed to hear that there was no longer any separation of race in the community of God's people (Ephesians 2:11-13).

Perhaps our churches need to hear and learn the same.

Case study: God's word cuts through cultural barriers

Ying grew up in an Asian culture where people would never speak out if they were unhappy or disappointed with someone else. To openly show anger or disappointment in others was not accepted. Instead, people would gossip about each other or not talk at all.

She became a Christian as a teenager, and would often share her faith in Jesus. One of those she shared with was a young soldier in the army who she met in a hospital during a visit to a sick relative. He also became a Christian – they eventually married, studied for ministry together, and became church leaders.

It was really tough working in a rural church – and there was much gossip, criticism, and underlying conflict which could not be addressed. People would never speak openly about anything that might lead to conflict.

Over time, they saw through God's word and working with western Christian workers that it is really important to talk to people when they gossip against us, and to talk to them face-to-face. If someone hurts us, it is our responsibility to go and talk to that person.

She saw by example that this way of dealing with sin could help people if it was done gently. This was very difficult at first, and went against everything that her culture had taught her.

But with God's strength and help, they slowly began to talk to people who had hurt them, and were able to gently put things right. God's word showed them a way to restore relationships.

Things to discuss as a team

Do you think that the Bible favours one culture above another? (Why or why not?)

How would you define a person who is "Spirit filled"?

What do they look like?

In the Bible, what does a person who is filled with the Holy Spirit look like?

Things to do (for team leaders)

Think of ways to encourage team members to read the Bible daily. Are there Bible reading notes and guides in their language that you can encourage them to use?

How can you use the Bible in team meetings to encourage team members in their walk with Jesus Christ?

Things to do (for team members)

How can you feed on God's word regularly?

What resources can you use to do so?

(For example, a Bible reading guide, sermons and Bible reading notes.)

Chapter 3
Choosing Team Members

What kinds of qualities do we need to look for in people who will contribute to a multicultural team? This list is designed to help team leaders choose team members – and to help each team member examine themselves.

Curiosity and engagement with other cultures

Good team members are going to show that they are open to learning about other cultures by their actions.

If you can see evidence that they really like to be with people who are different to them, then you can be confident that they will be able to work in a multicultural team. Some of the things to look for might include:

- a sense of awe and wonder at how our great God makes people so different and the world's cultures so diverse

- a positive attitude about learning and engaging with people from other cultural backgrounds (no, eating foreign food in restaurants a few times does not count!)

- friends from cultural backgrounds different from their own

- experience travelling to other countries, and engaging with the people there

- experience learning another language

- engagement in social activities or churches with people from different cultures

- a keen interest to explore information about other cultures – especially seeking to discover what is special about them

- an ability to critically examine their own culture, especially thinking about how an outsider would see their culture

Secure in Christ

People who are insecure will often react strongly when their expectations are not met. People who are self-assured can become arrogant and proud. People who are secure in their relationship with Christ have the advantage of recognising their own weaknesses and failures, and have their foundation in their relationship with God. Some of the ways that this can show itself are:

- a clear understanding of the good news of Jesus and the salvation that we have inherited by faith in His death and resurrection

- a deep sense of God's love in their life, to the point that it helps them through times of conflict and difficulty

- a track record of persevering through difficulty and pain, rather than moving on quickly when there is trouble and tension

- freedom from past guilt, so they don't blame themselves unnecessarily when difficult things happen

- resolved conflicts with others in the past, and not carrying bitterness and hurt from previous relationships

Humble commitment to God's Word

God's word is the foundation for any Christian ministry. Team members need to have shown that they look to the Bible for their guidance and direction in their lives, but also to be open to new ways of understanding it, as we look at it from a different cultural lens. Some of the qualities to look for are:

- a learning posture as they engage with the Bible – being open to hearing how others might interpret God's word in surprising ways, and expecting there may be points of disagreement

- a good understanding of and an ongoing commitment to reading the Bible regularly

Flexibility

A rigid inflexible approach will never work in a multicultural team. When expectations are not being met, the team member needs to be honest about that. If necessary, they might need to change their expectations, and be open to different ways of working together. Some of the ways that this shows itself are:

- flexibility with those areas that are not basic to the good news of salvation through Jesus (for example, the role of women, church governance, baptism, the Lord's supper)

- an openness to consider new ways of working and doing things

- an understanding of how different cultures shape a person, and a willingness to work with these

Once you have done an evaluation of a potential team member, it is helpful to give them some feedback about areas of weaknesses that you think may lead to tension within the team.

If you are aware of cultural or personality traits that might clash with others on the team, it can be helpful to raise awareness of these *before* they join the team.

For team leaders: Questions you can ask

As you talk with potential team members, you need to assess if you can agree on what is really important in working together.

How important is the Bible to you in your ministry?

What are your views about: the work of the Holy Spirit and charismatic gifts, the role of women, how we baptise people?

Can we agree to work together even if we have different views?

How much exposure have you had working together with people from cultures other than your own?

For team members: Questions for reflection/discussion

Ask other team members how they feel about your culture. Ask them to be really honest about the things that they like and don't like.

Ask your team members specific questions about their home culture:

- How did your family members relate to each other when you were a child?
- Describe your relationship with your parents as you grew up
- Describe how you lived when you were younger – rich or poor? Country or city? Extended family?
- Can you tell me about a significant event in your life during your childhood?

- Reflect on how you have related to people from different cultures in the past.
- What kinds of things did you appreciate about their culture?
- What things made you feel annoyed or frustrated?

Chapter 4

Team Preparation

Building an understanding of the people in your team and the cultural context that they have come from will help you to learn to work with them. You will find that the insights that you gain will help you to identify and avoid potential causes of conflict.

Our culture affects the way we approach life – the way that we work, our priorities, work/life balance, family relationships, and attitude towards money.

Learn as much as you can about the cultures of the people you will be working with. If you take the time to learn about the background and culture of others, you will be better equipped to interact with them.

It will help you to understand what has made others the people they are today. Even if you don't like what they do or how they do it, just understanding the reasons will help you to react appropriately.

Learning others' cultures will also help you to work through conflict, as you begin to understand how others think. It is also very hard to take offense at someone who is so interested in getting to know you and what your home culture is like.

People who grew up in places of war, poverty, and violence look at life differently to those who did not.

For some countries, like South Korea, the current generation of adults grew up during a time of rebuilding after a devastating war. They will have different values compared to someone who grew up in a very affluent society, such as some Western nations that have been prosperous and generally peaceful for more than one generation.

These differences in values can lead to tension between people of the same age, just as it caused tension between people of different ages in our own countries, between the generation that had lived through a world war and the post-war generation.

The best way to learn about each other's culture is to know each other as people first and to build a relationship based on trust and respect.

Case study: Having, having not

Josiah had grown up in a very poor family after war had destroyed their country. He was the third out of 4 children. The family owned a business and his father was often away, while his mother had to keep the business going in his absence as well as do all the house work. Josiah received little affection from his family and their lives revolved around work. When he was older, he had to help with the family business for no pay.

After becoming a Christian and being sent out to another country as a missionary, he was placed to work with a couple who came from a wealthier country. They seemed to have so much material wealth, and they also seemed to waste a lot of time watching movies, sleeping in and taking days off.

Josiah would regularly get up at 4am to join in prayer with other missionaries, but his co-workers would never go. He wondered if they ever prayed at all. They also seemed to be constantly struggling with so many things – language learning, the weather, relationships, discouragement. They would share openly about their difficulties – which did not seem that difficult to Josiah, compared to what he had to go through growing up and preparing for ministry.

At first he tried to be sympathetic, but after a few months it seemed that nothing was getting better. Josiah felt that they were quite weak, and wondered if they were at all suitable for his team.

Building deep relationships

Invest in quality time together. Talk together about your life, where you grew up, what were some significant events and circumstances in your lives that made you who you are today.

This is not something that can be done in one meeting. It may take an extended time – perhaps over a weekend retreat, time allocated during several team meetings, or sharing regular meals together.

In many cultures, eating together is a primary way for people to build enough trust to do business together.

Investing this time in each other is time well spent. It helps build trust.

When we trust each other, we tend to be more flexible when others do not meet our expectations, and more forgiving when they do things we might think is wrong or not polite. We may not fully understand how they think, but we decide not to be offended so that the relationship may grow.

Spending time together also helps us to work out things that might hurt others (much better to find out about this before rather than after we've offended people without wanting to!).

While it is almost certain that conflict will happen as the team forms and learns to respond and work together (because there are so many things that could possibly cause offense or conflict that it is impossible to eliminate them all!), there are things we can do as a team to make the process smoother.

Eating together is a great way to explore culture. Everyone eats food, but how we eat, and what we talk about while we eat, can be very different.

Koreans like to eat a meal together before discussing work. South Americans often talk and joke around over a meal for many hours before making a work decision. Westerners tend to get straight to the point when talking about work, then eat together (and not talk about work over the meal).

Where we like to eat together can also be different! While Asians tend to like to go out (often in big groups in noisy restaurants), Westerners tend to invite small groups to a pre-prepared dinner in a quiet home.

Share meals together in a few different contexts – such as your home, a picnic in the park, and a restaurant. Being willing to eat and talk over a meal in a way that is different to what we are used to can go a long way in building relationships.

Case study: Family time

Steve and Dianne went to a resort together with Sam and Elaine, who also brought their children for a few days. Steve and Dianne had a 2-year old who they stripped naked to play in the paddle pool, as they usually do.

Sam and Elaine were horrified. In their culture they would never allow their children to run around in public without clothes. They quickly took their children back to their room, where they spent the rest of the day without coming out to the pool again.

Steve and Dianne decided that they would not cause offense and that their children would wear a swimming costume when swimming in the pool.

Case study: A dinner party

Enoch and Grace had moved from a Western country to an Asian country and had learned enough language to begin making friends with the local people. This is Grace's story of when they invited some local friends over for a meal:

Early on, we were keen to have people over for meals at our place. We felt blessed with a good apartment, and we wanted to use it in order to build relationships with fellow workers.

So we bought ourselves the biggest oven we could find, thinking, 'This will be great for when people come over!'

For our first meal, we had a husband and wife over.

I roasted a beautiful chicken and made some salad, set up the table, put out the knives and forks...I was very impressed with myself.

They looked really awkward as they held their knives and forks. They had never used them before. I guess it's something we take for granted, but really, how difficult they are to use!

The wife went for her piece of chicken. We had never seen anyone eat the chicken so cleanly. She probably ate some of the bone. Look at the servings of meat from their cafeteria! That portion of chicken we gave them was probably how much meat they would eat in a whole week! No wonder the wife devoured it the way she did.

The husband didn't seem to touch his chicken. We thought that quite strange. He didn't seem that impressed at all.

(Looking back, it all made sense. When we learned more, it didn't surprise us at all that the husband wasn't impressed. It was because of the local culture. We thought we were giving him the best piece, the meaty chicken breast – but chicken breast is the cheapest bit. The bit they liked, the expensive bits – were the feet, the neck, the wings! AND they liked their chicken super spicy, with a dash of MSG and chicken powder for extra flavor – how bland and dry our chicken must have tasted to him!)

All of a sudden, they announced that they were leaving and suddenly left. So we watched them put their shoes on, said goodbye and closed the door.

And we sat there thinking, "That was weird!?"

It was only later that we learnt from our culture class and also the example of our local friends, that the polite thing to do is to 'send' people out. That is – to walk them out, to their car, at least down the stairs, and to the big door of the apartment complex. *The further you walk out with them, the more esteemed they feel.*

How rude we must have come across, when we just closed the door! How much we had to learn.

From that night onwards, we decided to invest in a hotpot. (The local people love it. They eat it in the sweltering 40 degrees summer heat.) And we decided to buy lots of chili, garlic, sesame sauce, vegetables, tofu and a little meat.

Wow, how different it was. People were familiar with it – they felt comfortable, and they stayed for a long time.

After a while we got quite sick of hotpot because it's not exactly good for you many times a week – but over these meals, our friendships with these local friends deepened.

How to learn about the culture of your team

- *Read books* about the culture of your team members, or stories set in their context and history. Sometimes reading can give valuable insights into other cultures.

- *Observe* the people from the same culture as your team members. It may be possible to join in their cultural activities, join in a church activity, or even visit their country if possible. Sharing cultural experiences with your team members will help you to understand them much better.

- *Ask questions* about their culture, background religion, families, friends, relationships – you only learn when you ask questions.

- *Learn some language*. This might take some effort, but it will give you a window into their culture. Language contains many clues into the worldview of each culture, and how relationships work. It also enables you to speak to the "heart" of your team member.

Things to talk to each other about

What does each member expect from the team? This can vary greatly. Some cultures expect a team to work like a family – with little privacy, spending both work and leisure time together. Others expect the team to only meet during a weekly meeting, with everyone working on their own during the rest of the week.

Some cultures expect to eat a meal together and have time talking about other things before talking about work, while others only want to talk about work, and do the jobs for which the team was formed.

When different cultures have such different expectations, it is easy to look rude or abrupt in front of people who think differently.

QUESTIONS TO ASK

Ask each other questions, listen, and talk openly.

- How often do you think we should meet, and where?
- What is an experience you've had with a team in the past, how did the team work, what was successful or disappointing about the team?
- What do you think should be our vision, mission, and strategy?

- How would you like to see decisions being made?
- What do you think we should do if we disagree, or when there is a conflict?
- If X (hypothetical situation) happened to our team, what would you find helpful, or how would you like to see the team deal with it?

Listen as others talk about their hopes and fears about what the team aiming for.

Showing trust and respect

How do we show trust and respect to other team members? Again, this can vary greatly between cultures.

Some cultures honour and respect each other depending on status and age. In some cultures it would be rude to question the team leader, but in other cultures it is quite normal to ask questions, and even challenge the leader. Others show respect based on work experience and competence.

We can show trust and appreciation in many different ways – such as giving a gift, providing hospitality, lending money, giving compliments, or visiting without being invited. How we do this varies between cultures, and can become a complicated game in which it is easy to make mistakes.

It can help a lot if we know how to show trust and respect in the culture of our team members, so that what we do will have the positive impact that we want to have.

For example, in Persian culture, a gift or an offer of food must be declined three times before it is accepted. For those to move to another country, it can be very difficult to adapt to another culture where food or drink is only offered once only.

(Many Persian migrants have gone hungry and thirsty because they have refused food and drink once or even twice without being offered again.)

If we are working with someone from a Persian background, then it is important that we offer food or drink three or four times to be sure that they don't want what we are offering.

Case Study: Building trust and respect

Julio and Chris had begun working on the same team, but came from different cultures. When people become friends in Julio's culture, they share things like their possessions, and even their money if their friend has a need. In Chris' culture, people become friends when they are willing to share their intimate thoughts and feelings.

After a few months of working together, Chris still didn't feel that he knew Julio very well – so he invited him over to watch a game of football, to give them some time to hang out together. When Julio came over, he went straight to the fridge and helped himself to some food and a drink – then asked if he could borrow some money before he left.

Chris felt offended that he still had not got to know much about Julio, but that Julio had just helped himself to his "things." Julio felt that his friendship with Chris was much closer than before, but was confused about why Chris seemed so reluctant to lend him money.

Being heard

How do we make sure every team member is heard? Even asking this question can be tricky.

Some cultures ask questions during team meetings, take turns to speak and listen, and give each person a certain period of time to talk.

Not every culture, however, allows everyone to voice their opinion. In some cultures, the team leader has the biggest voice, and team members do not speak up if they disagree. In other cultures, people do not openly say things they feel other team members might disagree with, and younger members may not speak at all.

It is important to provide ways for all members to be heard, so that the whole team can benefit from all ideas and experience – and to allow each other to give to the team in a way that is comfortable and culturally appropriate. Some options are:

- Speaking to a team member privately before a meeting to find out what they really think

- Writing down responses to a question on paper, maybe without revealing their name

- Going around the circle so that everyone has a chance to speak and give their opinion

- Giving people some time to prepare a response by writing it down before speaking

- Raising an issue, but being prepared to leave the decision until the next meeting to give time for the leader to hear everyone out in private

Julio was part of a company that sent him to an Asian country to work with an international team. His company made an agreement with an agency to take responsibility for him while he was working there and sent money to the agency to cover his salary. Under the agreement with the agency, he was working under "secondment." This meant that the agency had full authority over him in his work.

After a couple of years, the agency made some decisions about his work arrangements that he felt the agency did not have the power to make, and he was very upset. After talking further about the arrangement, and looking at the written agreement, Julio and the agency leader realised that the "secondment" agreement had been translated as "partnership" into Julio's language.

This gave a different meaning to the relationship. In Julio's language, there was no such word as "secondment."

Julio and the agency then had to discuss again their understanding of how much authority the agency had over him in his work.

Once this was done, a new and clearer agreement was made.

Things to try as a team

- Spend a weekend together to get to know one another.
- Share meals together in a few different contexts – home, picnic, and restaurant. Talk about how each of your home cultures uses food to build relationships.
- Talk about your expectations for the team. How often to meet? How would relationships work? What to do if there is tension or a conflict?
- Discuss how you build trust and respect in your culture.
- Talk about a leader that you really admire, and why you respect him or her.
- Talk about a team experience that you have had in the past. How did the team work? What was successful or disappointing about the team?
- Talk about vision, mission and strategy – and how you would see things working.
- Listen to others talk about their hopes, dreams and fears about what the team is aiming for.
- Discuss some hypothetical situations the team might come across, and how you might deal with them.

Chapter 5

Moving towards the Goal

Every team needs a purpose and a goal. How these goals are expressed can be quite different between cultures.

So often we take for granted what it means to work in a team. We may think that all teams that work well do so in exactly the same way.

It can be quite a shock when we find out that others have very different expectations (and experiences) of goals, leadership, and team-work.

Vision: Setting goals together

Some cultures like to begin with writing the goals down very clearly on paper so that everyone understands what the goal is. Other cultures find that writing the goals down is too formal and restrictive, especially when the language is difficult for them to understand.

Many cultures prefer the leader to set the goals and to live out these goals for everyone else to follow – these goals may not even be clearly stated, and progress towards the goal might depend on each team member's relationship to the leader.

Other cultures expect team members to spend a lot of time discussing goals, and come to an agreement before major decisions are made. This can be tiring and confusing for team members who don't understand or agree with the direction that the team is going.

If the frustration builds up then it can lead to an open conflict and division in the team.

When team members speak different languages, it is important to take the time to carefully explain what the team is meant to be working towards, and give time for discussion and reflection.

Often team members already understand and are committed to the goals before the team comes together, but we cannot assume this is always the case.

Sometimes words that we use in our explanations do not translate easily into another language and can have shades of meaning that are different.

Some ideas to help this process along might be to:

- Write down the important points on a board that everyone can see. This can help those who have trouble understanding everything that is said.

- Ask people if they would prefer to have a written vision and mission statement to help the team to move along.

- Give some time for people to reflect quietly individually, before giving everyone in the room a chance to speak.

- Ask people to write down their responses to set questions, and then read them out for everyone to hear.

- Have people split into small groups to discuss the goals, and then give feedback to the bigger group.

- Have the leader talk to team members privately around a meal, to try and listen to their thoughts that they may not be willing to say to the whole group.

- Be prepared to delay making an important decision, if you are not sure that everyone agrees with what is being proposed.

- Try to come up with vision and mission statements that describe in simple language what your goals are and how you are going to go about reaching that goal. Even if some team members don't find it helpful, it will help you to stay on track for future reference.

Case study: Dealing with frustration

Nick and Mary were sent from the UK to work in a team under the leadership of an Indian couple. A single woman from the Philippines was also on the team.

Nick was feeling discouraged because the previous team that he had worked in did not have clear goals. This team also did not have clearly set out goals and a strategy that he could agree with. Because he felt that he had said too much in the previous team that he had worked in, he decided to mainly keep quiet in the new team.

Things did not improve for Nick, and after a few months, he felt that he could not put up with the situation anymore. He felt that everything was very unclear. He did not know exactly where he was supposed to fit into the team, what he was supposed to be doing, or what goals the team was working towards. He felt that the team discussions also lacked direction and not much was being achieved.

One day in the team meeting, he exploded with frustration and let the rest of the team know how he felt. The others were shocked by his emotions and raw honesty. They retreated from discussing their emotions openly, although they felt hurt, and did not really understand why Nick felt the way that he did.

A few weeks later, Nick and Mary left the team and returned to the UK, feeling that they had failed as overseas Christian workers.

Question for discussion: How could Nick have dealt with his frustration in a more constructive way?

Strategy: Working together towards the goal

How do people work together towards the goal, when each person is used to working one way according to their own culture? Each person might be working towards the same goal, but want to walk down different paths towards the goal. Often there will be disagreement about how to get there. One person wants to use a lot of money, another wants to do a particular activity – yet another is more focused on relationships instead of programs or activities.

Conflicts can easily happen. Working towards agreement, while giving people some flexibility, can take a lot longer than we might expect. Working together well involves good and frequent communication between team members – a lot of discussion about strategy, how to work together, and the vision of what the team is working towards.

Some issues to discuss include:

- How much money to spend? How is team money to be raised and used?
- How directive or inclusive should the leader be?
- Who should be included in the leadership team?
- How are team decisions made?
- What activities should be carried out and in which order?
- How do we work together?
- Who will do what?
- How often should the team meet together and for how long?
- How will the team socialise together (if at all)?

Case study: Same heart for outreach, different ways to reach

Jo, Dan and their families decided to work together to plant a church. They both had a clear goal of starting a new church in an area where there was no church at all. They spent a lot of time together to talk about what kind of church they wanted and what it would look like. Once the team had agreed on the goal, they then clarified certain aspects of the strategy such as when to employ a local pastor, how big the congregation would be before the team began to pull out, the time frame for reaching certain goals.

It seemed that everything was going well – and after a few months a few local believers had joined them, as well as a few new Christians. A group was starting to form. The time came in their first year when they began to plan their Christmas outreach.

Jo came from a cultural background where parents and bosses put on generous parties to show their love for their families and employees. He wanted to organise a big, expensive party – and pay for all the expenses.

Dan came from a culture where people are more independent – so he felt that the small group should take responsibility for the outreach program and costs. He felt very uncomfortable with the way Jo was organising the outreach.

First, Jo did all the organising without including the local believers in his plans. Then he wanted to spend a lot of money on food, entertainment and gifts. Dan knew that they had the money in the bank to cover the expenses, but he thought it was not good to spend it all on the outreach, because it would not help the church later when the original team moved on.

Dan felt that a large party would start a precedent that would cost too much money for the local church to continue when they left. Jo felt that since the money was there, they had an obligation to put on the best party that they could with the money that they had, otherwise it would not show that they cared for the church.

Neither would give up their point of view, and eventually a big argument broke out.

Question for discussion: How would you help Jo and Dan resolve their differences?

Evaluation: Reviewing goals

Every team goes through changes.

When there are changes inside the team or outside the team, a review is necessary to respond to the changes.

If a team member leaves, then all the resources of that team member might be lost. The team can no longer use the member's knowledge and skills in the same way.

If a new team member joins the team then there needs to be a discussion about where they fit into the team and what their role is going to be.

If the ministry situation changes, new goals need to be set that respond to the new situation.

Team members might need to change their roles, or work together in new ways so that the team can continue to be effective.

Ideally, when these changes happen, there are already good relationships between team members. An open discussion about goals is helpful only after good relationships have been made.

Multicultural teams: an exercise in grace

There can be times when it feels that working in a multicultural team is like walking through a field full of landmines. There are so many different values and expectations which can clash at any time.

Sometimes we may think our team is working well together, and then all of a sudden a conflict can occur that takes everyone by surprise.

As this can be very unsettling for the team, we need to respond with grace and maturity.

It is important to try and isolate the issue and to determine which cultural values may have clashed to cause the conflict.

Sometimes conflicts can be caused by a clash of personalities, but more often than not they are caused by different cultural values.

Case study: Changes in teams

Hernandez was a professional soccer player and had joined a team which consisted of South Americans and Japanese people working together. Hotaka was his team leader and came from Japan.

Hernandez did not feel comfortable in the team and their direction and requested a transfer to another team which was more in line with his own vision. Thomas was his regional leader and discussed the possibility of a transfer with Hotaka on three occasions.

Since Hotaka had not raised any opposition to the transfer, after a period of about 12 months Thomas approved the transfer by email, sensing that it had the approval of everyone involved.

A year later during a personnel review, Hotaka expressed his disappointment and frustration to Thomas that the transfer had gone ahead without his approval or consultation. He felt that Thomas should have spent much more time engaging with him on the issue before he made the decision to approve the transfer.

Thomas was surprised because he felt that he had talked about it enough, and that the decision had the approval of everyone involved.

Hotaka explained that his expectation was that much more consultation and listening should have taken place before such an important decision was made.

Things to do – for team leaders

Prepare a set of goals together with the team.

This may include: a vision goal (what you would like to see achieved) and a mission goal (what you hope to do as a team). Work on this over a period of time, so that it becomes a statement that everyone can agree to. Discuss it both in the meetings and privately. Talk about how they see what they are working towards.

What do you see the team working together to do?

What does success look like to you?

How long do you think that this might take?

How do we decide when our work is finished?

Develop a strategy of how you are going to work towards your vision (this is a plan of how the team will achieve the goals that you have set).

What will you do?

When will you do it?

How will you do it?

Which order will you do it in?

Who will do what?

Where will it be done?

Why will you do it there and then?

How often and in what way will you measure progress?

Chapter 6

Communication Styles

How we communicate with each other can bring our team together or break us apart. It is not just what we say, but also how we say it that is important.

We need to pray and think very carefully about which form of communication is best to use in each situation.

Once we have built trust within the team, we then need to understand the best ways to communicate with our team. This can be like a delicate dance where balance and timing become very important.

It can be hard to decide.

Do I write a letter or meet face-to-face?

Should I make a phone call or text a message?

Do we send out a policy document or talk together about the issue?

Should we talk individually to each person first or talk to everyone at the same time at a meeting?

How do we overcome language barriers so everyone understands clearly what others are saying and have agreed to do?

There are no easy answers to these questions.

Different cultures have different ways of talking about different issues. Conflict might be dealt with one way; a major decision about strategy might be dealt with in another way.

In some cultures, issues are talked about privately and informally – so when the time comes to meet together, the decision has already been made and agreed upon. Other cultures prefer to talk about an issue openly in a group and people say what they think – even if they disagree with someone else. Some don't like to write down agreements – others do.

Understanding how each team member prefers to talk about an issue will help teams move forward without tension building up. Leaders can give members an opportunity to talk about how people communicate as a team in their home culture.

Case study: Ways of communicating

Tom had been working in a multicultural organisation for about 7 years, when he received a letter one day from Heidi, who he had known and worked with on a number of different projects.

The letter was a complaint about his behaviour and listed 6 different actions that he had taken that had offended her. Tom felt that some of the accusations were unfair, and some he could not even remember. His first thought was to write back to defend himself. After praying about it, Tom felt that meeting together would lead to a better result.

A few months later, he was able to talk through the 6 points with her and her husband, and found out that the issues that she had brought up were not the real problem.

The real issue was that she had been hurt by an email Tom had sent 5 years earlier – an email which denied her request for financial support for her children. Although that issue had been worked out with her husband, she still felt resentful, which led her to express her emotions in a letter 5 years later.

Heidi preferred to write letters whenever she had a grievance, but in the end the issue was best resolved with a personal meeting involving her husband. If Tom had responded in kind with another letter, the issue may not have been resolved.

Face-to-Face

When meeting face-to-face, it is important to know how issues should be discussed before discussing them.

For instance, I found out too late that Korean people like to eat a meal first and then talk about work issues.

I found that some Brazilians will sit around and tell jokes for hours before they get to the point of a meeting.

Thai people may not discuss the issue directly but express their views indirectly – which means that the listener needs to listen very carefully (they also smile a lot, even when the conversation is serious).

Europeans tend to be very direct and open about their feelings – but this can often cause hurt and deep feelings of anger. Such directness may sometimes lead to damaged trust and relationships that may break up a team.

I have found that in most cases it is best to meet face-to-face when there is anything important to talk about that involves emotions. This is because:

- it is easier to understand how they feel

- it is easier to clarify things that you don't understand

- it is easier to see if the other person understands what you have said

- it gives you the opportunity to respond to the other person quickly

- it can be easier to say some hard things face-to-face

- apologies can be made and misunderstandings cleared up more easily

- it gives you the opportunity to identify any fears, negative feelings, or opposition – and respond to these immediately

To keep emotions in check, it is helpful to have another person present who can be a witness, and help clarify what was said.

What if some cultures express their emotions

a this is a biased view

It is always best to remain calm and in control of your emotions, even if you feel frustrated and angry. Showing negative emotions will usually lead to a negative result.

Telephone calls

In some circumstances, telephone calls can be more effective than a face-to-face meeting.

For example, when a difficult decision has been made, it can be helpful to have some distance so that the other person does not lose face so publicly.

It is also still possible to interact on a deep level over the phone and to get instant feedback about how someone is reacting to an idea or a decision.

However, when using the telephone, sometimes we think we have communicated clearly – but our team member hasn't understood us at all!

This is because:

- we cannot see the other person's body language

- it is more likely that language barriers will get in the way if both are not comfortable with the common language used

- it is much harder to verify if the other person understands and agrees to what is being said

Case study: Verbal clues on the telephone

When Ruth had a leaking tap in her house, she phoned a Filipino plumber to ask if he could come and fix it the same day since it was an urgent job. After some hesitation, he agreed to come in the afternoon.

The afternoon came and went, and Ruth felt very upset that he did not come as he had agreed. It took a Filipino friend to explain to her that his hesitation indicated that he was not available, but he agreed to her demands because he did not want her to lose face.

Ruth quickly learned to pay more attention to pauses in the conversation, and to make requests using different questions.

Emails, text messages and letters

In a multicultural team, it is important to write short and clear messages, so that those who don't normally speak the language can understand with little effort. Try to write plainly, and ask someone to read your writing to check if it is easy to understand and to remove any words that might offend.

There are several advantages to using the written word to communicate:

- it is efficient – it does not require the other person to be available at the time you send it

- it is convenient – the other person can respond to your message when they choose to

- it may be easier for people who are not proficient in the language used – they have time to process what is being said and take their time to understand, than if they were trying to listen to spoken words

However, for issues involving people's feelings, it is best to avoid email, text messages or letters if possible.

When people start to send emails or letters full of emotion, it is very difficult for people to understand one another.

It is also very difficult to take back written words that may have offended someone.

It is also ideal to avoid the written word when communicating complex issues with someone who is not confident with the language used – another email may be just too much, they may find it hard to read (especially if it is too long, or not written plainly!), and they may not read it and not tell you (in order to save face, or to not be any trouble to you).

Case study: Team communication

Frank had worked as an accountant before he joined the ministry team. His previous work reflected his detailed personality, which he brought into a very diverse team.

Whenever there was a team meeting, he would take meticulous minutes of the discussions.

After the meeting, he would send out long emails with minutes and appendices which would explain the decisions and direction of the team.

Every team member was asked to spend time each month to fill in a detailed report of the activities that they had been involved in.

Most of the team members who had not been to English-speaking schools groaned under the burden of reading long emails, and having to submit reports so often, in a language which they found very difficult.

After six months, Frank realised that the team members were not reading his notes and most of them were not submitting reports on time or not at all. The reports that were written often did not make much sense.

Frank decided not to get angry and changed his expectations.

Instead of pushing them to submit written reports, he would visit the team members in their homes – or call them on the phone at least once a month to ask them how they were doing and discuss current team issues with them. The only meeting notes he sent out were very simple bullet points of what was talked about and the decisions made.

He made an effort to slow down his speech during meetings, simplify and clarify issues in simple English, and give more time for people to reflect and respond when a decision was made.

This increased participation, and the team began to function much more effectively than before.

Chapter 7

Team Meetings

Meetings can be a great tool to inspire the team and make decisions. When done well, they inspire people with a passion towards the vision and to keep going despite the obstacles; they encourage through God's word, singing, and prayer, so that each team member grows in Christ and brings glory to Him. Let's work through some of the elements of a great team meeting:

God's Word

Every Christian team needs to spend time around God's word. Not everyone, however, learns from God's word the same way. Often, the style of reading and learning from God's word reflects the style of the education system in that culture.

Some cultures interpret, discuss and teach the Bible in a group, where debates are encouraged to explore different interpretations and points of view.

This style of learning may not work in some cultures where it is expected that the teacher will give the meaning and application of the Bible to people's lives. With this style of learning, people will mainly listen, and not ask many questions or give many answers.

Many cultures teach the Bible through telling stories and narrative since they were not able to read the text for themselves. In fact, much of the Bible is story, and for much of history, people would tell each other stories from the Bible and learn lessons from the stories.

It is important to find a method of learning that team members find meaningful, and that helps them to grow in their understanding of God's word.

Some options include:

- Textual Manuscript method – for more information, visit: http://rezchurch.org/wp-content/uploads/2010/10/IVGCFScripture-Manuscript-Bible-Study-InstrPDF.pdf
- Bible Story Telling method – Christine Dillon's *Telling the Bible through story* describes this in more detail

The group leader needs to understand something of the background and learning style of the team so that he can prepare the teaching in a way that can be received well.

Some useful questions to ask when preparing the Bible teaching might be:

- What language should we use with the reading and Bible study?

- Is the passage too long or difficult to read out loud for the team?

- If the leader does most of the talking will the team understand him?

- Would it be helpful to tell the story or read the passage?

- Are any visual aids or study guides needed, to help the team understand better?

- Are the questions easy to understand for the team?

- Are there any questions or issues raised that might make team members feel embarrassed?

Worship and prayer

Worship and prayer are crucial in setting the direction of the team towards God – the purpose of the team is to glorify God, not just to work towards the task that has been set.

It can be difficult to worship in a way that is satisfying for everyone in a multicultural team. People may be used to different styles of worship, and singing different songs in different languages.

And while all may desire to worship God, not everyone may want to sing or not everyone may want to sing the same songs.

Some will not enjoy singing songs they don't know in a language that they are not comfortable with. Some will enjoy singing traditional hymns, some will enjoy modern hymns, and some will enjoy contemporary praise songs.

Fortunately, many Christian songs are now sung widely all over the world in many different languages, so it is easier now to find songs that most people like to sing.

How we pray also tends to vary from culture to culture.

Some teams pray out loud all at once. Others pray one at a time with varying levels of intensity and body language. Some love waking for early morning prayer meetings, staying awake for an all-night prayer meeting, going to a prayer retreat on a mountain, going to a church or in a silent place alone (or with others). Some find it important to spend time alone with God while others feel the need to pray with others each day.

It is important to talk as a team about how each member likes to worship and pray, so we can understand how we can encourage people to grow in their relationship with God.

It may not be that everyone is completely happy, but in the end there needs to be some agreement about the style and content of the worship and prayer which most people can be comfortable with.

Language

It is essential that everyone understands what is being said.

A common language needs to be agreed on. In a multicultural team, it is likely there will be members who are not as proficient in the common language as others. In this case, the following may be helpful:

- *Allow time for silence and reflection* before team members respond. Silence can be uncomfortable for some, but for others it can help them understand, reflect, and think about a response – and then express themselves more clearly and more politely.

- *Take things slowly.* Don't rush through the agenda or talk too fast. I often see leaders with lots of cross-cultural experience forget to speak SLOWLY in a multicultural group so that others can follow.

- *Clarify* different points of view and reword the responses of team members, to help people understand what is being said more clearly.

- *Write the main points* on a board for everyone to follow. This can help team members see and process what they have heard and what others have said.

- *Form small groups for prayer and discussion.* Those who are not confident in the common language may feel more comfortable to express themselves in smaller groups. These groups could even be based on language, if appropriate.

- *Let everyone know that you are still open to feedback* even though the meeting is finished and it seems that a consensus has been reached on a decision. It may be that you have people who want to say something but feel too shy, or feel they haven't organised their thoughts and words enough to share right away. But they do have an opinion and it is worth listening to it.

Formality

Expectations about how formal meetings look could vary across cultures.

For instance, for some it would be disrespectful to God and other team members to wear shorts and T-shirts to a meeting, or to hold it informally on someone's lounge floor. For others, a more relaxed setting helps them talk openly about important issues.

It would be helpful for team leaders to talk to members individually about what their expectations might be. Even if you don't follow all expectations, this would give you insight into what team members are adjusting to and assure them that they have been heard.

These include:

- How structured should the meeting be?

- What should team members wear to the meeting?

- Where should the meeting be held?

- How should the meeting agenda (what you talk about at the meeting) be set? Who decides?

- Should the team members be told ahead of time what will be on the agenda?

- Should we take minutes (notes of who said what, and what was decided at the meeting)?

- Should we send the minutes to everyone on the team? When should they be sent?

Case study: Multicultural Team Meetings

Bijay was feeling very excited. He was sitting in the first meeting of a new multicultural team that he had been invited to join. The team was composed of people from all over the world with many different backgrounds. Over the next few months they would be working together on a new project which had been initiated by the team leader.

He had felt it a privilege to be asked to join the team, and his wife had agreed to move the whole family to a new town so that they could become part of the team. The people that he had met so far seemed very nice and easy to work with. Bijay had very positive feelings that the team would work well together and have good understanding of each other. Each of the other members had expressed the feeling that God had clearly led them into the team and that their role on the team was a good fit for both their passion and the skills that God had given them. Bijay felt the same.

In their first meeting together, the leader led a time of introductions and introduced the mission and vision of the team. There was quite a bit of discussion in trying to clarify the strategy of how they were going to move ahead.

At first, Bijay appreciated the way that some of the younger team members were able to express their views, and the team leader was listening and trying to help them to see that his way forward was the best.

But after some time, Bijay became uncomfortable – he felt that some of the younger ones were expressing their views in a way that was disrespectful.

One young man openly challenged some of the leader's decisions and said openly that he did not agree. Bijay would never dream of speaking like that to his leader, so he stayed quiet and said nothing. Even some of the women were more outspoken than he had ever seen before.

While the team leader did not seem threatened by their challenges, Bijay felt that they were not behaving appropriately and should address their concerns in a private meeting with the leader. To do it openly seemed like a loss of face for the team leader.

Over the next few months his discomfort increased.

He noticed that some of the open disagreement led to some good decisions being made by the team. In most cases it did not seem to create ongoing tension within the team, but he still felt as if people were not treating each other with enough respect.

Sometimes a young team member would call older people by their first name and even tease the team leader about his clothes. The Caucasian members of the team would sometimes wear shorts to their meetings, which he felt was quite inappropriate. While the team leader did not seem to mind, it made Bijay feel very uncomfortable because a young person from his culture would never behave so informally in a work situation.

The final straw came when Bijay's wife started to challenge his authority at home. She began to express her opinions in much the same way that the wives and young women did in the meeting. The first time this happened, he felt humiliated and angry that she would challenge his authority as the man of the house. When he thought about the negative effects the team was having on his family, he began to think seriously about leaving.

Frequency, length and start time

Another way in which cultures often differ is their concept of time. Expectations can vary greatly.

Some may feel it is important to meet and pray for one another, even if nothing is achieved at the meeting. They feel that maintaining relationships is the most important thing.

Others may feel frustrated by this and wish to meet only when there is a task that needs to be done or a decision needs to be made.

People have different expectations about being on time even within their own culture, so when some people are habitually late, it can become a source of tension within the team.

It is important to talk to each team member about what they think about the following:

- How often should the team meet?

- What is the purpose of meeting?

- How long should the meeting go for?

- When (day, time) should the team meet?

- What happens if some people arrive late?

- How far ahead of time should the meeting be organised? (For example, one week before the meeting? One month?)

Case study: Planning a meeting

Pastor Somchai was the leader of a denomination of 40 churches scattered around Bangkok. About once a year he would have something important to discuss with the pastors and missionaries working among their churches.

In these cases, he would call a meeting for the following week and expect everyone to attend.

Pastor Somchai would often get frustrated at the western missionaries – because most of them would often give the excuse that they already had appointments for that day and therefore would not make themselves available to come to the meeting. While all the Thai pastors would cancel their scheduled appointments to attend his meeting, the western missionaries would not.

Somchai felt that their attitude was disrespectful and that they should make their leaders a priority instead of their calendars. The western missionaries' view was that an important meeting would be planned further ahead so that they could attend. If it was only planned a week ahead, then it must not be important enough to bother attending.

Participation

It often takes time and effort to engage team members so all feel they are heard and contributing to discussions.

Team leaders also face the challenge of juggling different cultural expectations. In some cultures, the team leader is expected to do most of the talking – in others, the team members are expected to do most of the talking.

Giving each person a chance to talk in front of the whole team might help – but it might make team members lose face if they don't have anything to say or feel that they have said the wrong thing. It is therefore important that the leader of the team meeting encourages everyone to have a say.

Some ways to do this could be:

- *Have a break* before team members give their feedback so that they have some time to think about what they might say.

- *Ask for some feedback in pairs or small groups first* so that people can express their views.

- *Ask people to write down their thoughts.* Often team members can write down things more clearly than they are able to say them.

[handwritten: What if it's someone from a high power distance culture]

Variety

Team meetings do not have to run the same way every time! You can pray differently, worship differently, structure things differently and ask different people to lead. Multicultural teams have plenty of varied experiences and cultures to draw from for new ideas!

Remember that even if the team has started doing things one way, and it is working well, it does not mean that other ways will work badly – they might work just as well, maybe even better.

Variety brings many benefits:

- When each team member has an opportunity to run a meeting, others in the team get a good idea of what the member's expectations are, and what they enjoy

- Team members learn, "Other ways of doing things may work too!"

- Team members learn about each other

- Team leaders gain creative ideas for how meetings could be run

Fun

Having fun together builds trust and relationships within a team.

Yet what is fun can vary from culture to culture.

Ask each other what you do for fun! Try some different activities to see what people enjoy doing together – this could include eating, playing sport or board games (not competitive – competition may make some people uncomfortable as there are winners and losers), cultural activities, team challenges...

Trying something new might be more fun than you thought – and trying something that is fun for another team member (though not necessarily fun for you) will help build relationships in a way that is worth a little discomfort.

What is important is that you are growing to understand and appreciate one another, and this will help the team in the future.

Food

For some cultures, enjoying food is an essential part of meeting together. For others, it can be a distraction that they feel is unnecessary.

The truth is that most cultures are pretty attached to their idea of good food, and this can also be appreciated by others if they are prepared to try something new. So be prepared to try some new flavours.

It is important to sense how valuable this might be for some people and for all team members to be willing to share a meal together as part of the process of building team relationships.

Eating together is a way for people to build relationships across most cultures. Even if the team does not eat together during every meeting, it may be helpful to organise a meal during some meetings to give people more time to talk during an informal setting.

Children

People from different cultures may have different views on how children should be included. Some cultures may want to include the children in team meetings or have them play while the adults are talking. Others may want the children to be separated or put to bed early in the evening.

Either way, most parents are sensitive to being criticised about how they bring up their children, so it is much better to discuss where children fit into the team before this question becomes a problem. Waiting until it already is a problem may more easily lead to hurt feelings.

Things to do as a team

Use some different cultural practices in your team time together:

Try out different foods from each team member's country as snacks or even a meal.

Try out different customs from home churches – a different way of doing Bible reading, prayer, preaching, Bible study, or singing, with each team member leading the time.

Have a time where people pray in their mother tongue (with translation if appropriate)

Discuss with the team how often it is appropriate to meet and what the team members hope to achieve by meeting together.

Chapter 8

Dealing with Conflict

talked abt by
Hibbert?

Every new team will go through 4 different stages. These are: forming, storming, norming and performing. How quickly a team will move through these stages depends on a number of factors such as:

- attitudes toward cultural differences
- personalities
- team preparation
- flexibility
- people skills
- ability to forgive
- ability to negotiate cultural differences

Not every team will experience open conflict, but there will always be some tensions that will need to be resolved if the team is to grow close and work well together.

Usually these differences can take us by surprise. It can be very comforting to know that even very effective Christian workers such as Paul and Barnabas had a very strong disagreement which broke up their team (Acts 12).

So don't be discouraged if tension breaks out. Use it as an opportunity for people to grow to appreciate and understand other people's cultures and values.

Case study: New roles

When I first started a leadership position in Bangkok, there were some people who were very generous and came to my office with expensive gifts. I had known them for years as a co-worker, but now that I had a leadership role it seemed as if my status had risen to a new level and they wanted to honour me in the new role. Since I come from a European background, I found it a bit strange, but also nice that they would treat me in this way.

Stage 1: Forming

The team is coming together, and relationships are still new and fairly superficial. Everyone is nice and polite to each other and trying hard to be accepted and not cause offense. They are getting to know each other and are working to develop a deeper level of trust as they do.

At this level, everyone is careful to avoid hurting each other, and usually quick to apologise if anyone has misunderstood or been offended.

Case study: Bonding with new team members

Jim had always thought of Filipinos as outgoing and very warm people who loved to be in community. However, when Julio and Maria arrived from the Philippines to join his team they were very different to what he thought. They seemed quite withdrawn and private. Many of his invitations to spend time together over a meal or to go out on a social event were rejected.

At first he felt upset and confused because they were not behaving at all as he expected. Over time he realised that they were going through some very difficult adjustments to the new country and they felt very homesick. They were also much more quiet and introverted than most Filipinos that he had met before, so he had to learn to adjust his expectations.

After some months of working together, he felt that they had become friends. He found that not judging them and taking more time to get to know them helped him to avoid tension.

Stage 2: Storming

This is a stage that comes a few months down the track when relationships are established.

It is at this stage when routine behaviours can become annoying and cultural differences can begin to cause tension.

People can begin to feel resentful when they feel ignored or not responded to as they had hoped.

This is the dangerous phase – if emotions explode, they can cause a lot of damage to the team, perhaps even destroy it.

In multicultural teams, it can be very difficult to handle tension in a way that leads to deeper trust and understanding.

For instance, in some cultures it is acceptable and desirable to address conflict directly, even sometimes showing anger and frustration.

In other cultures, showing such anger and frustration in front of the whole team is seen as aggressive and unacceptable, and equivalent to hitting someone physically.

It takes a great deal of wisdom, strength and insight to handle these situations and it will not always lead to a happy ending.

Stage 3: Norming

If the storming stage can be dealt with well to diffuse tension and conflict in a constructive way, then the team can move into the "norming" stage.

This is the point where most of the hardest points of tension in relationships have been dealt with and the team is growing to accept one another's differences.

There may still be hurt feelings from time to time but there is a growing understanding of each other's cultures, backgrounds and personalities.

There is a growing commitment to accept one another, to accept each other's weaknesses and faults, and to work together to honour God in spite of these.

There is also a growing humility and recognition that our actions can hurt others. We each try to change our behaviour in such a way that other team members feel more comfortable with us.

Stage 4: Performing

The team begins to really perform when trust and commitment are demonstrated to each other.

At this point the team can begin to work together in unity.

Each member has learned to recognise each other's weaknesses and has some insights into their own. Each team member will hopefully feel a sense of privilege and gratitude towards the team and a genuine appreciation for what other members bring towards the work.

Is it Really Worth it?

Before we begin to work on a project, we should ask the question, "Is forming a multicultural team really worth it?"

It can take a lot of emotional energy to go through the 4 stages of team formation.

My experience is that for many adult teams, it often takes about 2 years or even longer before the team reaches what could be called a "performing" stage.

If it means bringing a team together from very different cultures for a time of less than 3 years, then it may not be considered to be a good investment of time and effort. If the team is going to spend 2 years learning to work together for 1 year of effective ministry, then it may be better to look at other ways of achieving the goals and task that the team was meant to achieve.

Another way might be to form a team of people who are more similar in their cultural orientation, even if they are not from the same country. It will depend on the type of project, the age of the team members, and how closely the team members will be expected to work together.

There needs to be an assessment done to determine whether the effort of forming a team will lead to effective ministry. Some questions that can help in the assessment are:

- What resources are available that will help the team to function well? Is there organisational support to help the team?

- Would team preparation, training and regular assessment by an outside consultant help the team to perform better more quickly?

- Are the personalities and preferred working styles of the team members compatible and flexible enough to work together?

- What are the possible changes in team members over the life of the team? (For example, retirement, home assignments, resignations, medical problems.)

- How consistent will the ministry situation be while the team is working together?

Conflict Resolution

Dealing with building tension in the team before it breaks out into open conflict is usually the best way. Strained relationships are not always obvious in a team, so it may not always be possible to see it.

Sometimes we hide our feelings or pretend they are not there.

Sometimes we express anger and frustration because of another problem in our lives, not because of anything our team has done, such as childhood trauma, a family problem, or cross-cultural stress.

A multicultural team should assume that tension and possibly open conflict will occur at some point during their time of working together.

Just as different types of fires are put out in different ways (it would be a big mistake to try to put out an electrical fire with water for example!), each conflict needs to be dealt with differently with each person involved. Assuming that each person will want to resolve a conflict in the same way can make the conflict worse.

When we have been hurt and offended we tend to think, "What would I do in my home culture?"

And each culture has a different way of resolving conflict.

Some feel that talking through the issue face-to-face, and then apologising if necessary, is the best way to resolve a conflict.

Others would prefer a mediator to help, and not meet face-to-face.

Some would consider a gift an appropriate way to reconcile.

Others feel that a long time is needed before the relationship can be restored.

Some prefer writing letters or emails to avoid seeing someone face-to-face, or because they feel they are better able to express themselves clearly in writing.

To know how to interact with each person in a conflict situation takes a great deal of skill, tact and grace.

One thing that can help is for the team to make a plan as to how to resolve conflict *before* any conflict happens.

Jesus gives us a good plan in Matthew 18:17-19. If we are offended by someone, it is our responsibility to first go to them and talk to them about it. Many conflicts would be resolved if Christians used this plan.

It is really hard to go to a person who has offended you and talk about the issue with love, but it is the only way to clear up the misunderstandings that will happen in a multicultural team.

If there are team members who would find it too hard to do this then it can be achieved through a mediator who is trusted by both sides.

If each team member commits to following a plan for resolving conflict, it can help to ease feelings of offense and resentment within the team.

Each team member is accountable for following the process.

Case study: Friendships and conflict

Grace had travelled to Japan in order to tell Japanese people about Jesus. The first year was really tough and lonely, but in her second year she began to make friends with the ladies that she was sharing a house with.

On one occasion Grace made plans to go out with her housemate, Haruna. When Grace was invited to another event on the same day, she talked with Haruna about changing the plans that they had made. Later, she found out that she was able to change plans for the other event so that she could be with Haruna as originally planned.

Although there was no change in their plan, Haruna was very upset.

When she spoke to Haruna, Grace found out that Haruna was upset that she hadn't been 'apologetic enough' when Grace had suggested a change of plan. She was so angry that she was seriously thinking of ending their friendship.

This was a big shock! Haruna's expectation was that Grace should have been more apologetic, according to Japanese manners.

At first, Grace felt hurt that Haruna might end their friendship over such a small thing. But another Japanese friend helped Grace to realise that it was because Haruna cared deeply about the friendship that she was willing to talk to her about it (in Japanese culture, conflict is often avoided, and Haruna's openness meant the relationship was very important indeed!).

In the end, the friendship was restored. Grace was able to apologise with more understanding so that Haruna was happy. They visited Haruna's hometown together and had a wonderful time as close friends once more.

Things to do as a team

Work together to outline the process of what team members will do when they feel offended.

Read Matthew 18:17-19 together and talk about how Jesus' words might apply in your team.

How will they communicate with the person they have been offended by?

How will the offenders respond when they find out that they have caused offense to someone else?

Chapter 9

Team Change

Daniel and Gloria planted a church in a large Asian city and appointed a young pastor to lead the church. It had taken 5 years and much hard work.

When they went on Home Assignment for a year, they handed the church over to Sam and Frances to work with the local pastor while they were at home.

During the year, a new couple joined the team, and were working well with Sam and Frances. Sam had a heart for the poor people living in the slum community near the church.

When Daniel and Gloria returned after their Home Assignment, they were not happy with the way that Sam and Frances had been leading the team and asked them to leave. They wanted to take back the leadership and return the focus of the church to student ministry.

Sam and Frances were then forced to move out and begin a new ministry a few kilometres away. They felt very hurt to have to move on from the team.

The changes in leadership and direction caused a lot of chaos and turmoil in the lives of everyone who were involved.

Sometimes teams work well for a while – and then something changes.

This could be a change in leadership, someone leaves, a new person joins the team, or some unexpected event happens – and the way the team works together can change completely.

The team may have been stable and functioning well for some time – and when someone new comes in, all the old ways have to change.

Sometimes this can be exhausting and cause new conflicts. There can be grief and loss, or even a breakdown of morale.

How can the team keep working together well when something changes?

When there's a change of leadership

Every leader will have a different style of leadership and set a different direction and goals for the team.

This can be tiring for the team members who have become used to working one way and now have to change. It can upset the relationships in the team as everyone has to adjust.

Having interim leaders can also be very tiring and confusing, because their leadership is not permanent and people know that more changes are coming when the interim leader moves on.

Case study: Leadership loss and humility

Simon and Elaine were working in a team with another married couple and a single young man. They were all in their early thirties and worked really well together as a team. They shared a similar cultural background, even though they came from different countries. All had lived in the Asian country they were in for less than 4 years, so they all shared a sense of learning the language and culture together. Simon and Elaine led the team, and Simon especially enjoyed the sense of responsibility and direction he was able to give.

After a year or so of working together, a couple who had been working in the country for over 20 years joined the team. Simon was no longer the team leader and no longer the best language speaker on the team.

He felt a sense of loss and disillusionment. He had to learn to give up control to the senior couple.

The team vision remained the same but team meetings completely changed.

The transition was difficult, but over a few months the team became able to adjust to the new situation, and Simon committed himself to work under the leadership of more senior and capable leaders.

He discovered the meaning of Paul's words, "Do nothing out of rivalry or conceit, but in humility consider others as more important than yourselves." (Philippians 2:3)

When a new person joins the team

Most teams will have people leave and new people join. This is normal and can be due to many different reasons.

The team needs to understand that changes *will* happen, and that resisting change will not help the new people who have joined. Everyone needs to be flexible and welcoming of the changes that need to be made.

A new team member will need to be brought into the culture of the team that has already been established. They will bring their own home culture into the team and will need to learn about the cultures that each person on the team brings with them as well.

To do this, some of the lessons of Chapters 3 and 4 need to be applied all over again in choosing team members and training the team.

There needs to be a process in choosing a new person, assessing their suitability, and then making a decision as to whether they should join or not.

They will then need some training to be able to fit into the team.

Every time new members join the team, team dynamics change. New members will have a relationship with each of the existing members. They will have their own cultural assumptions and expectations. They will also have assumptions about the role of the leader, what it means to be a team, how decisions should be made, what the strategy should be, how meetings are held and how people should relate to one another.

If the new members are not leaders of the team, it would be helpful for the team leader to go through the goals, vision, and mission – for the benefit of the new members, and to reinforce it with existing team members.

While the team vision may remain the same, it may well be that plans will need to change, as the team learns to work with new members. Flexibility and commitment to the vision during this time of change is vital.

Case study: Natural Disaster

When I was working in Bangkok, the Boxing Day Tsunami of 2004 caused many deaths in South Thailand among Thai people as well as tourists. Our team had a number of people working in South Thailand, and many of them helped people to recover from their losses.

The purpose of the team from the beginning was to plant new churches. Now they found that they had to re-evaluate their goals. As they changed their methods to help in the disaster relief they found many opportunities to build new relationships with local Thai people.

In the end, there were a number of Thai churches started in the area because our South Thailand team was flexible enough to change their strategy to help Thai people when the disaster struck. Being flexible and able to change led to many new opportunities.

When a person leaves the team

Losing a team member can lead to a real sense of loss as the resources and relationships of the person who left are now gone.

Sometimes members may even feel the team is no longer able to function. Often there are emotional attachments to the people leaving, and different cultures may show this sense of loss in different ways.

During this time, the team leader has an important role to play to help the team through the process of coping with the loss and moving on. People from some cultures find it helpful to talk about their feelings, while others need space and time to adjust in their own way. Everyone is different.

Sometimes the loss of a team member means gains for the team!

As the remaining members reflect on how to move forward, they may adopt new and creative ways to fill the gap. Other team members have the opportunity to try new things, and changes may be made to their roles that are a better fit for their personalities and skills.

People change as they go through life stages, and it may well be that some members are seeking to contribute to the team in a new way or to take on a new task. Team change can be a positive experience if it is managed well with a positive outlook.

Changes of circumstances, strategies and goals

Changes can be difficult, but they are at times necessary. Sometimes teams are compelled to change because of the changing environment around them.

There are always changes going on around us – such as changes in people and customs, technology, politics, and business. Some of these may not affect the team direction at all.

However, there are other changes that the team needs to be aware of, and that might require the team to change what it's doing. It is important to recognise that different cultures respond to changes in a variety of different ways.

This does not mean that they are wrong. For example, Japanese culture is more group oriented, and changes may take longer to make. However, these changes can be more effective because the change would only be made when all in the team are in agreement. And when everyone is in agreement, each person will work to make it happen.

This is in contrast to more individualistic cultures, where an individual might choose to change without the consent of the team. This may help others to change, or it can cause division with those who don't agree.

In other cultures, the leader may simply tell people to do things in a different way without discussion.

The team needs to recognise that in a multicultural team, change might be approached in a few different ways.

It is important to take time to listen, pray and discuss the changes with each of the team members before they are implemented.

Change in a Christian team

No team is going to stay the same forever, but Jesus is the same yesterday, today and forever. He is the one who will supply our needs as we seek to please Him and commit to doing things His way. We can trust that He is providing – and will continue to provide the resources and the people to do the work that He has called us to do.

When changes are negotiated successfully with a dependence on God for His provision for the ministry, the team can and will move forward into the future.

Things teams can do when changes happen

When a new member joins the team:

- Welcome them with a multicultural meal from the team members. Ask each team member to contribute something from their own culture.
- Talk about the vision and mission with the whole team.
- Define the role of the new team member in relation to the rest of the team.
- Talk about the vision and mission with the new team member to make sure that they understand it.

When a team member leaves the team:

- Give them a good farewell to show appreciation for their work on the team.
- Take time to acknowledge the emotional side of a team member leaving. If they have left under negative circumstances then it may take some work to find healing in order to move on.
- Assess the strategy and goals of the team to see if they are still realistic.
- Talk with the remaining team members about their roles into the future.

When the circumstances outside the team change significantly:

- Be open about the changing circumstances so that others can have input into what changes are necessary.
- Assess the original vision and mission to check if it is still relevant.
- Evaluate the strategy and goals of the team to see if they are still realistic.

For personal reflection

Recall a time when you had a conflict with someone from another culture. Did you feel that you acted with grace and forgiveness?

Would you have done anything differently today?

Were there any biblical principles that applied to your situation?

Did you grow in your relationship with God through the experience?

Conclusion

Citizens of His Kingdom

Multicultural teams have the power to influence our societies and show the power of God over and above the kingdoms of this world. Our faith in Jesus is more important than our nationality, language, or cultural rules. Our new identity is in Jesus – we are citizens of His Kingdom, and this is more important than our identity in this world.

We have in fact become aliens and strangers in this world as we live out our new identity and become transformed into the likeness of Jesus (1 Peter 2:11). If we can live this out in a team with others who are from different backgrounds, then this would show that God's power in our lives can bring people from all cultures together.

It will become a model of what we will be one day in heaven.

Choosing to work in a multicultural team is choosing to do what is difficult. It is much easier to work with people who have the same background, culture and theology as we do.

By making a choice to work with people from very different cultures we are intentionally choosing to interact with different values and ways of getting things done.

This has the power to change us and the way that we see the world. This transformation does not come easily, however.

Sometimes God will teach us some painful lessons along the way as we try to work together with people who come from a different cultural perspective to our own.

At times this can make us feel bruised and battered, as we face conflicts and tensions that we did not expect. We may not always fully understand why these painful misunderstandings have taken place.

But God did not call us to an easy and pain-free ministry. Working in a multicultural team means accepting that there *will* be pain, as we try to work together.

There will be times when we will need to apologise for the way that we offend other people, intentionally or unintentionally. We may need to work in ways that we don't feel entirely comfortable with or do not really enjoy.

But in all this, we have the hope that God will use us as a team, as we seek to work together for His glory.

God bless you as you go forward with your team.

Made in the USA
Columbia, SC
31 July 2020